101 Flirting Tips for Women and Girls

How to Flirt With Guys, Be Confident Around Men and Carefully Use Your Body Language to Attract and Pick Up the Guy You Want

Shawn Burns

www.ShawnBurnsBooks.com

ISBN-10: 1460919211

ISBN-13: 978-1460919217

Reproduction or translation of any part of this work beyond that permitted by section 107 or 108 of the 1976 United States Copyright Act without permission of the copyright owner is unlawful. Requests for permission or further information should be addressed to the author.

Neither the author nor the publisher assumes any responsibility for the use or misuse of information contained in this book.

Copyright © 2011 Shawn Burns
All Rights Reserved.

Printed in the United States of America

Table of Contents

Introduction..1

Chapter 1 - The Basic Steps of Flirting With a Guy..3

Chapter 2 - How to Flirt With a Younger Guy 23

Chapter 3 - How to Get Into a Guy's Head..33

Chapter 4 - How to Flirt With a Guy Without Looking Easy 39

Chapter 5 - How to Pick Up a Guy 49

Chapter 6 - How Teenage Girls Can Flirt 67

Chapter 7 - How to Flirt With a Guy on the Phone 75

Chapter 8 - The Finer Points of the Art of Flirting 91

Chapter 9 - How to Act Around Guys to Make Your Flirting Successful 97

Chapter 10 - How to Overcome Shyness Around a Guy You Like 109

Chapter 11 - How to Flirt and Drive a Guy Wild 119

Chapter 12 - Dress for Success When You Want to Flirt 127

Chapter 13 - Where to Flirt 135

Chapter 14 - Tips for Flirting Appropriately for Your Age 143

EXTRA HOT Information – More HOT Tips for You Here..............................151

Introduction

Flirting is used by many women who want to meet the kinds of guys who might possibly be their mates and to learn fairly quickly if they are at all compatible. At times, you may attend a dance or a party and notice a man you are interested in, but may not see again. Flirting can increase the likelihood that you will see an interesting guy again in the future and may even lead to a romantic relationship.

The art of flirting is an interpersonal skill, and it can make you nervous at first. Fortunately, flirting can be learned. This book has many tips to help you become more comfortable with flirting and help you meet the man of your dreams.

Chapter 1

The Basic Steps of Flirting with a Guy

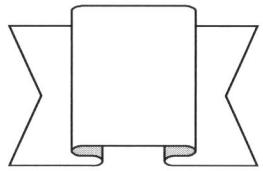

101 Flirting Tips for Women and Girls

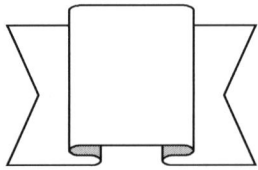

Tip 1

Have fun.

You should enjoy flirting. But in order to enjoy it, you need to reduce any unrealistic expectations you might have. In many cases, flirting is not serious and just a fun thing to do for a short time. It is possible that you might not talk to a guy again after you flirt with him, either by your choice or by his choice. Just get out there and flirt with another man. Don't be disappointed if you don't hit it off with a guy you are flirting with. Sometimes, flirting may lead to a date or a loving relationship, but sometimes it won't. Remember, you're just flirting.

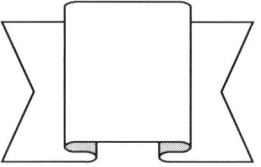

Tip 2

Be approachable.

Put a smile on your face and relax. Your body language is important for giving a guy the impression that you are fun to be with. Take a deep breath and don't be nervous. Be confident and your confidence will reflect itself in your body language.

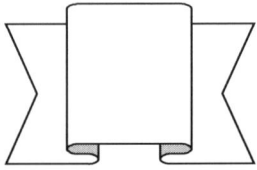

Tip 3

Check out a guy's body language before you start flirting with him.

See if he appears to be approachable. Is he looking your way and does he look like he is interested in you? You can continue to monitor a man's body language to confirm whether he is still interested in you.

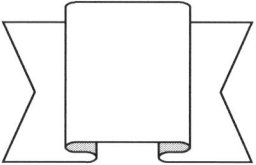

Tip 4

Make eye contact with a guy for a couple of seconds, but don't stare at him.

Give the man a fast and confident gaze, and look away from him slowly. Now look at the guy again and see if he is looking at you. If your eyes meet, then he may very well be receptive to more flirting.

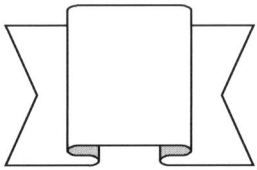

Tip 5

Start a conversation with the guy.

You can begin with small talk if you don't know the guy. Share an observation with him. You could simply say that it is a nice day or you could say that the bar, dance hall or other place you are at is really crowded. Just try to keep your observations positive so you don't sound like you are complaining. It doesn't really matter too much how you start the conversation. If the man gives you a positive response, then continue with the conversation. If the guy appears to be uninterested, he may not be receptive to further flirting, so watch his body language closely if you want to keep flirting with him. Play it safe to begin with, and don't talk about personal things just yet.

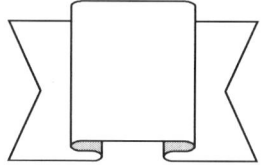

Tip 6

Begin to share personal information.

Ask the guy about himself and share things about yourself as long as the small talk continues to go well. You and the man you are flirting with may want to formally introduce yourselves so that you can call each other by your first names. Try to open up gradually and don't share too much information too quickly. Feel free to include more small talk and observations in your conversation to keep the conversation going.

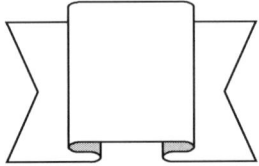

Tip 7

Make sure the guy has your complete attention.

Laugh at his funny remarks or jokes and try not to be distracted by your environment and the other people around you. Listen to what the man says and look like you are interested in listening while he talks.

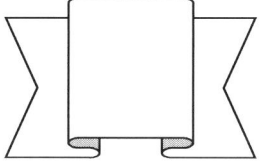

Tip 8

If you want to get romantic, show it with your body language.

    As long as your conversation continues to go well, you might want to touch him. You could briefly and gently touch his arm while you are talking. This kind of touching helps break into his personal space, and most men tend to be open to being touched. But proceed with caution, and stop getting physical if you get negative signals from a guy.

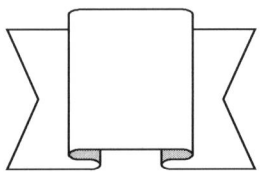

Tip 9

Go further.

In many cases, flirting doesn't go beyond your initial conversation. But sometimes you will want to see a guy again in the future. You may be interested in finding out if you would enjoy spending more time together. Don't plan too far ahead yet, but start with exchanging phone numbers or email addresses.

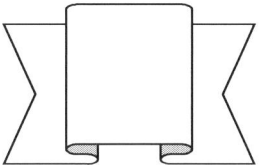

Tip 10

Keep your conversation lighthearted.

Have a fun conversation. Just try not to say anything dumb or idiotic.

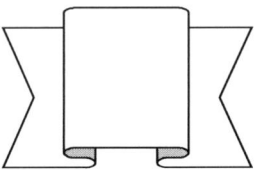

Tip 11

Refrain from talking on your phone or texting while you are having a conversation with a guy.

Show him that you are more interested in talking with him than in talking to someone else who is not there with you.

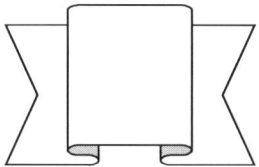

Tip 12

Try to stay away from discussing any of your unique interests for too long.

Continue to talk about your interest if a guy has the same interest or he asks questions about your interest. Be polite and try to strike the right balance between talking and listening to a man.

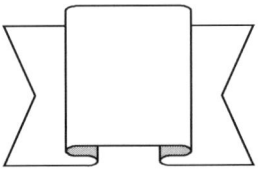

Tip 13

Try to avoid appearing as needy.

Keep your conversation light and positive and don't let him know that you will be disappointed if things don't work out between the two of you.

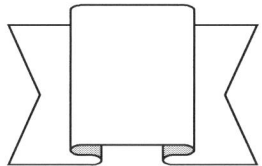

Tip 14

Be sure not to lead a guy on if you are not romantically interested in him, unless you are certain that he is not romantically interested in you.

After leading a man on, you may have embarrassing or uncomfortable experiences that could have been avoided.

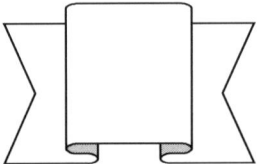

Tip 15

Be sure to only flirt in locations where flirting is an acceptable behavior.

Workplaces are usually not a good place for flirting, and flirting at work can seriously undermine your career in many cases.

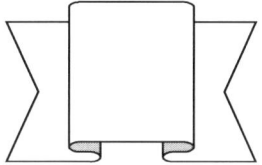

Tip 16

Avoid dirty jokes.

Try to avoid telling jokes that may make a guy uncomfortable or give him the wrong impression.

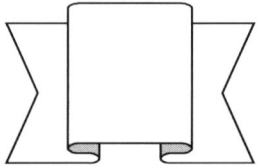

Tip 17

Complaining is a turn off.

Keep the negative vibes out of your conversation or you may end up depressing a guy or pushing him away.

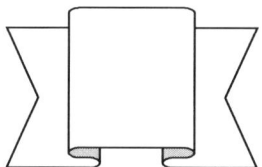

Chapter 2

How to Flirt With a Younger Guy

Many women like to date younger men. Older women often have more fun with younger guys because these men generally have more fun than men who are older. Women who flirt with younger men usually try to appear more sensual in order to better attract younger men.

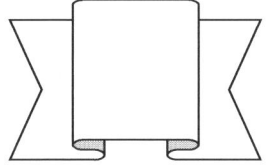

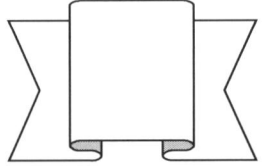

Tip 18

Be a sexy dresser.

Your appearance is important. Stay in good physical shape with regular exercise. Dress with fashionable clothes that show off your body. Walk with confidence and poise.

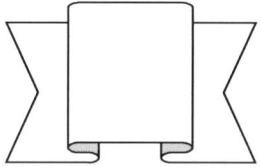

Tip 19

Use the right body language.

Make eye contact with a guy and use lustful and playful glances to keep his interest. Flip your hair in a sensual way. Smile softly and laugh when necessary. Touch him while you laugh.

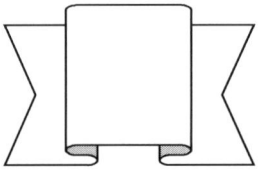

Tip 20

Younger men like the confidence that older women exude.

Be confident and humorous and try not to take yourself too seriously.

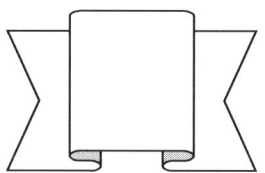

Tip 21

Share funny stories and experiences that reveal how smart you are.

But don't bore a guy with stories about your job, your children or your ex. Give the man a chance to speak and listen to him intently.

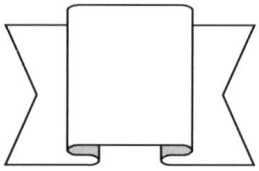

Tip 22

Don't be a nag.

Younger men are turned off by older women who nag them and try to mother them. The guy already has a mother. Show the guy that you feel secure with him.

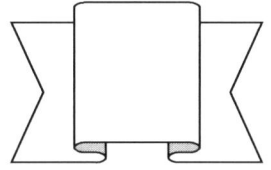

Tip 23

Don't appear to be smarter than a guy.

Show a man that he is interesting and that his conversation is stimulating. Try not to give a guy the impression that he is inferior to you or less intelligent than you. Make him feel special.

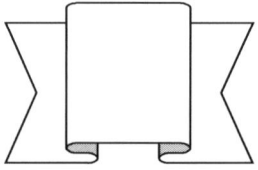

Tip 24

Learn from your experiences.

Use your past relationship experiences to be strong and mature. Be secure in yourself and younger guys will appreciate it.

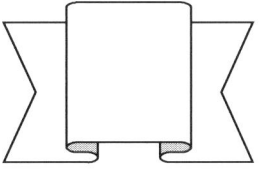

101 Flirting Tips for Women and Girls

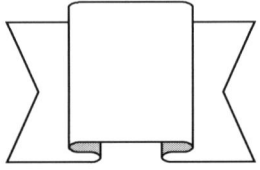

Chapter 3

How to Get Into a Guy's Head

101 Flirting Tips for Women and Girls

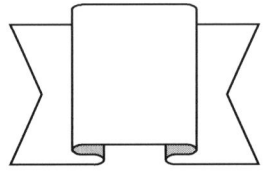

Tip 25

Exchange glances.

You can often get intro a guy's head by exchanging several glances with him. Look at how a man reacts to your glances to see if you are having the desired effect. He might give you a coy and sexy glance. A guy may also smile at you quickly. He may also turn his body to face you. If you get these kinds of feedback, you may want to proceed with further flirting.

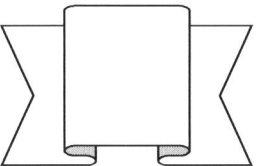

Tip 26

Touch him.

Give a guy an innocent touch on him arm during a conversation, especially if you are laughing at one of his jokes. He may return the move and give you an innocent touch on your arm or shoulder.

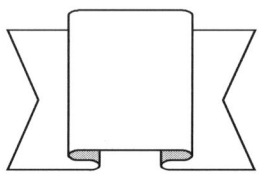

Tip 27

Mirror his behavior or see if he mirrors your behavior.

See if a guy crosses his leg after you cross your leg, plays with his hair after you play with your hair. Does he touch his face after you touch your face or does he shift his position after you shift your position? These are clues that the man is subconsciously paying attention to you.

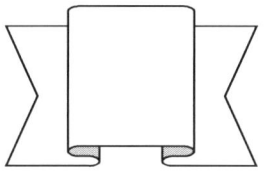

101 Flirting Tips for Women and Girls

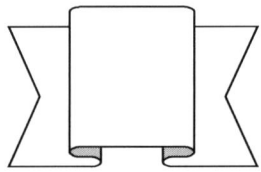

Chapter 4

How to Flirt With a Guy Without Looking Easy

Subtlety is the key to flirting with a guy and not coming across as being easy.

101 Flirting Tips for Women and Girls

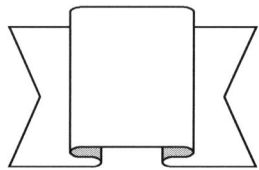

Tip 28

Use coy glances.

A brief but coy glance with a little bit of a smile can often be used to communicate your desire to a guy.

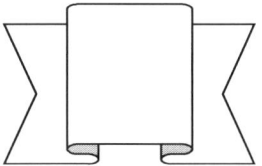

Tip 29

Speak softly.

If you speak more softly than in a normal conversation, a guy will instinctively move closer to you. Speaking softly can sound sexy and seductive to many men, especially if you hesitate a little while you talk.

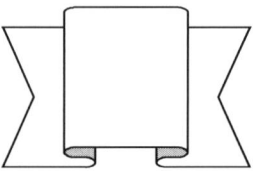

Tip 30

Have a bright smile.

If you give a guy a bright smile with your full face you will usually brighten your face and give him a positive vibe. This is especially effective in letting him know that he is special.

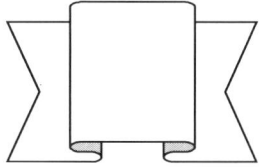

Tip 31

Tilt your head.

A slight tilt of your head can make you appear to be a bit shy. By combining a head tilt with a coy glance or smile you are sure to get a guy's attention.

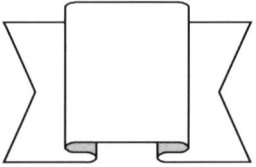

Tip 32

Laugh.

You can boost a guy's ego by laughing at his silly remarks or at his jokes. Just try not to overdo it with the laughing.

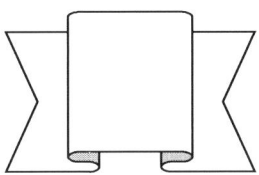

Tip 33

Pick on a guy.

Picking on a guy just a little bit can remove a lot of the tension between the two of you. If a man is offended you can tell him you were only joking. Strong guys will usually be able to handle a little picking.

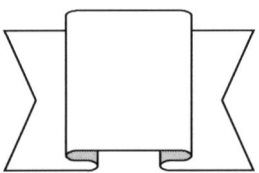

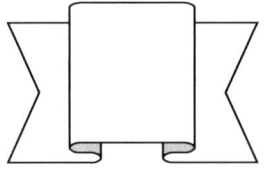

101 Flirting Tips for Women and Girls

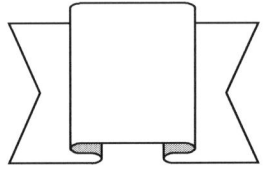

Chapter 5

How to Pick Up a Guy

101 Flirting Tips for Women and Girls

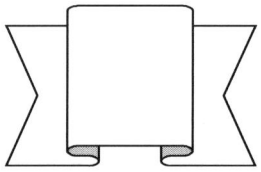

Tip 34

You don't need to just sit there and wait for a handsome guy to introduce himself to you.

Go ahead and pick up the man you want and go about it the right way. Of course, you should try to make sure he is single first.

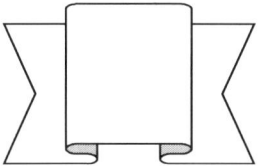

Tip 35

A bar may not be the best place to pick up a guy if you want to see what kind of person he is.

Lots of men act differently after a few drinks than they do when they are sober.

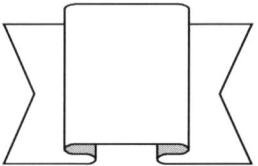

Tip 36

Some women have success meeting guys online through social networking sites or dating sites, if you are into that sort of thing.

But at some point you will need to meet the man face to face to get to know him in ways that you could never do online.

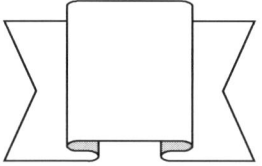

Tip 37

There are many different places to find guys, just pick a good spot for you.

Check out the men at the park the next time you go there for a walk. Look around at the store and you may be surprised at the guys who are shopping there. If you like art, then try scoping out men at art galleries or museums.

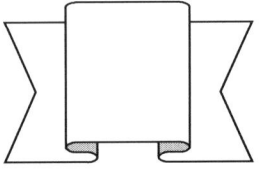

Tip 38

Some locations tend to be hot spots for guys to hang out.

Gyms and health clubs, computer stores, and even coffee shops can be excellent spots to find lots of men.

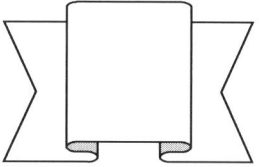

Tip 39

Once you notice a guy you want to meet, you can start flirting from a distance to get his attention.

Smile, make good eye contact and look approachable. Be sure that your feet are pointed at the man you want to meet. Avoid crossing your arms or your legs as these gestures can give a guy the impression that you are closed off and don't want to be approached.

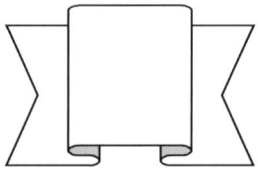

Tip 40

Learn about a guy through conversation.

You're going to have to talk to a man at some point in order to get to know him. You can learn a great deal about a guy by listening to what he has to say, and you can even learn if he has any undesirable characteristics such as bad breath. If a man is not for you, then it is much easier to end this chance meeting than to wait until you are on a date with him. You can simply tell him that you have to go, or that you need to make a phone call, say good bye or tell him to take it easy, and end the encounter right there.

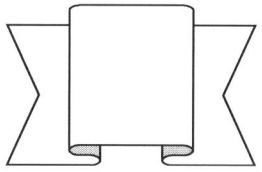

Tip 41

If you like the guy, then close the deal.

If you want to see him again, you can give him your phone number and end the encounter. In some cases, you may want to give him your email address in addition to your phone number or instead of your phone number.

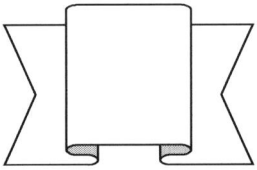

Tip 42

Be bold.

If you see that a guy has been glancing in your direction and checking you out for a while, walk up to him and ask him if he would like to take you out. Give him your phone number and ask him to call you sometime.

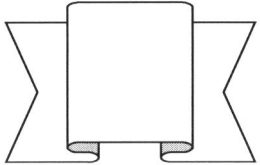

Tip 43

If you want to be a little more discreet, ask a waiter in a bar or restaurant to give a note to a guy that you like.

Write in your note something such as "Let's hang out soon" or, "How about having coffee sometime?" Perhaps, you could also include a complement in the note such as, "I like your shirt."

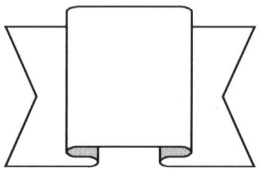

Tip 44

Some guys may be nice and take your note, but they might not call you back.

They may be shy, they may be interested in other women or they may just not be into you enough to ask you out. But don't take it personally if you don't hear back. Just keep on flirting with other men and you will have a guy asking you out in no time at all.

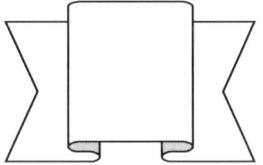

Tip 45

Guard your privacy.

If you are hesitant to give out your full name or phone number, just give a guy a throwaway email address that you only use for strangers which does not include your full name. You can give him your cell phone number instead of your home phone number.

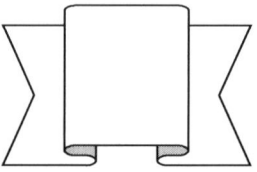

Tip 46

Watch a guy's expectations.

A guy might assume that you are easier because you picked him up. Be sure to draw the line on what you find acceptable if he gets too pushy or too steamy for you.

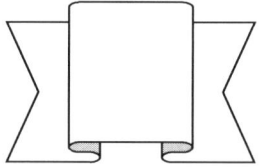

Tip 47

Guys might be less secure with your flirting if you are out with a group of other women and these women are watching the whole encounter.

This can make your flirting targets a bit intimidated. Tell your girlfriends to control their giggling and other types of behavior that may embarrass a man.

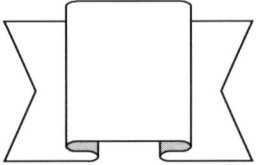

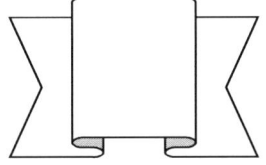

101 Flirting Tips for Women and Girls

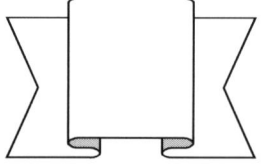

Chapter 6

How Teenage Girls Can Flirt

Flirting can be frustrating for teenage girls. But with a little practice, a teen girl can learn to flirt successfully and get to know guys more easily.

101 Flirting Tips for Women and Girls

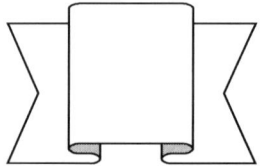

Tip 48

Smiling is important.

Your warm smile makes you appear friendly and shows a guy that you are interested in him. If you want a man to notice you, start by smiling at him.

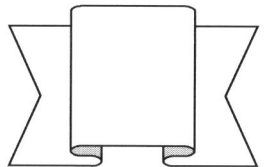

Tip 49

Look at him and make eye contact.

Try not to stare or overdo it with the eye contact. Just give him a brief glance until your eyes meet for a moment.

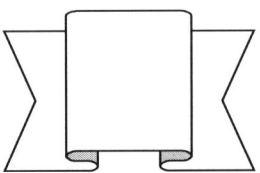

Tip 50

Talk with him if you are interested.

Ask him about his interests. Compliment him on his taste in music or his clothes. Be enthusiastic about what he is talking about without being over eager.

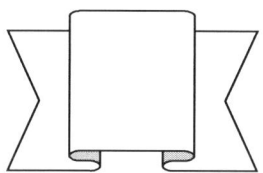

101 Flirting Tips for Women and Girls

Tip 51

Don't be phony.

Just be yourself and your natural confidence will shine through. Being yourself also helps you to know if he likes you for who you really are.

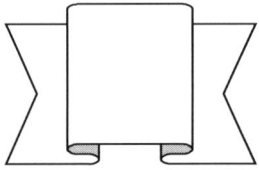

Tip 52

Keep it subtle.

Don't overdo the flirting or you may come across as trying to seduce a man. Be discreet and subtle and your veiled signals will often cause a guy to be more interested in you and want to get to know you.

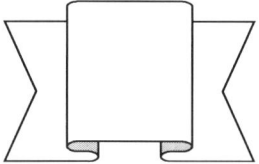

101 Flirting Tips for Women and Girls

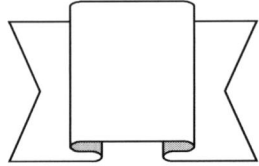

Chapter 7

How to Flirt With a Guy on the Phone

Phone conversations are a great opportunity to flirt with a guy. You don't have to sit there in awkward silence if you follow a few tips.

101 Flirting Tips for Women and Girls

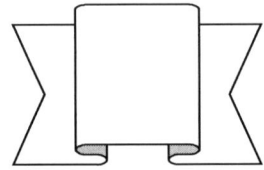

Tip 53

First, you need to relax.

Have fun when you speak with a guy. Don't be uptight or tense. Take off your shoes and wear something comfortable to help you be yourself while you talk on the phone.

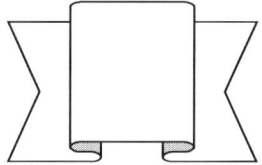

Tip 54

Avoid topics that can raise your stress or anxiety levels.

Stay away from topics such as how much money you each make, how many kids you each want to have, religion and politics. You could talk about the weather if you find yourself drawing a blank during the conversation.

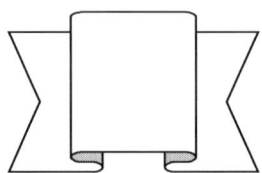

Tip 55

Try to get the guy to talk about himself.

An easy way to do this is to ask him what he is doing at the moment. Ask him what he enjoys doing, his hobbies, pastimes and interests. You can ask follow up questions or statements such as "That sounds interesting, tell me more about that."

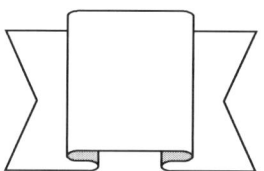

Tip 56

Compliment him.

Stroke his ego by laughing at his jokes or his witty comments. Tell him he is a good listener if he is reserved and lets you dominate the conversation.

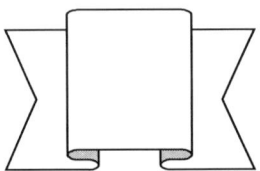

Tip 57

Talk about your shared experiences.

If you have both attended past events or gatherings, talk about your experiences. This helps build a common bond between you and him. But avoid experiences that bring up negative emotions.

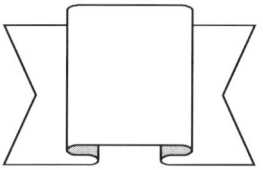

Tip 58

Plant images in his head.

Talk about your body in a subtly suggestive way without getting into phone sex. For instance, you could say that you have been working out and have lost a few pounds.

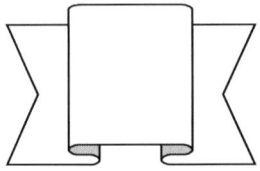

Tip 59

Make plans.

Tell him you would like to speak with him again soon. If you feel like dating him, you could say that you would like to see him again and spend time with him. You could schedule a date or arrange to see each other at a future event such as a party.

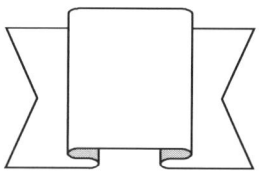

Tip 60

Don't be distracted.

Eliminate any distractions that keep you from concentrating on your phone conversation. Turn off the TV, stereo or radio. Don't sit at your computer while you talk.

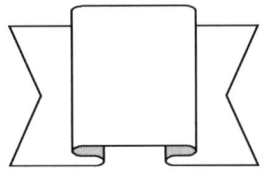

Tip 61

Don't eat, drink or chew gum while on the phone.

Chewing, lip smacking and burping can be distracting in a negative way.

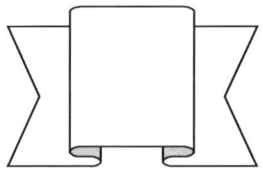

Tip 62

Be careful with teasing.

Too much teasing can be a turn off.

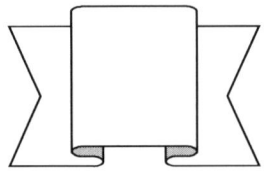

Tip 63

Don't argue with him or insult him.

Keep the conversation civil.

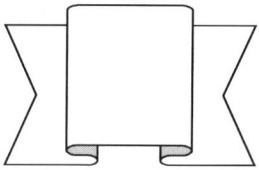

Tip 64

Don't monopolize the conversation.

He may get bored if you don't give him a chance to speak.

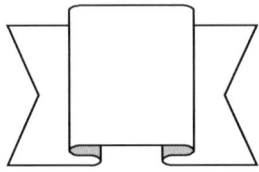

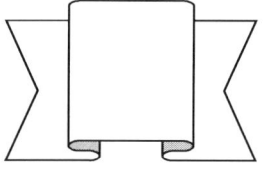

101 Flirting Tips for Women and Girls

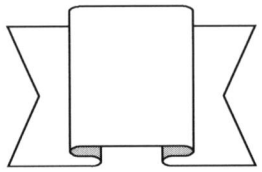

Chapter 8

The Finer Points of the Art of Flirting

Tip 65

You don't need a supermodel's body or the prettiest face to flirt effectively with a guy.

Be confident in your body and your appearance. A confident and positive attitude can be very attractive to a guy.

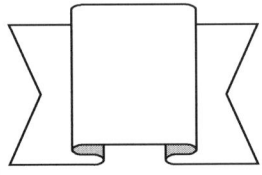

Tip 66

Accentuate your good points to draw his attention away from your problem areas.

You can show off a little bit of cleavage, but be sure to leave enough to his imagination or you will look like a tramp. A pair of jeans that fit you just right can bring attention to your legs.

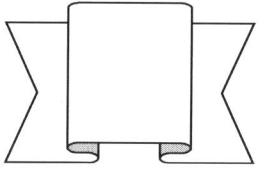

Tip 67

Make a guy your hero.

You can try the dumb blonde approach, even if you are not a blonde, to get a man to help you out of a jam. This can boost his ego and lead to more playful flirting. Just try not to overdo it with this approach or the routine may become tiresome.

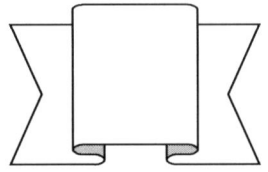

Tip 68

Drop a pen.

You can drop a pen and slowly bend over to pick it up. This can make you appear just a bit naughty and attract a guy's attention.

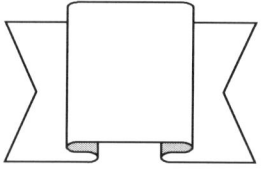

101 Flirting Tips for Women and Girls

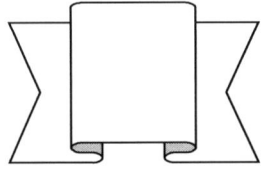

Chapter 9

How to Act Around Guys to Make Your Flirting Successful

101 Flirting Tips for Women and Girls

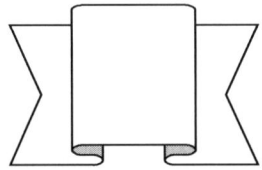

Tip 69

Meet a guy's friends and get to know them.

This way you will not be a total stranger to a guy you are interested in. Be kind to his friends.

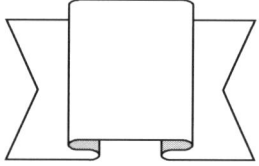

101 Flirting Tips for Women and Girls

Tip 70

Don't ask others to ask a guy if he likes you.

This can make you appear to be desperate.

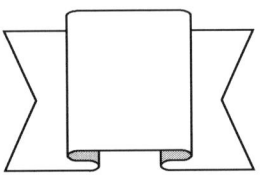

Tip 71

If a guy doesn't pick up on your subtle flirting at first, try flirting with him another time.

It may just take him a little more time to notice your interest in him.

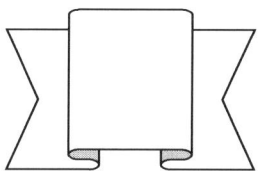

Tip 72

Address a guy by his name when you speak with him.

Most people like to hear their names.

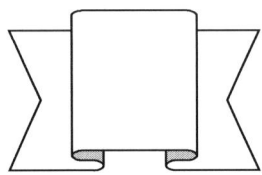

Tip 73

Act like yourself.

Don't act like you are better than him or that he is better than you.

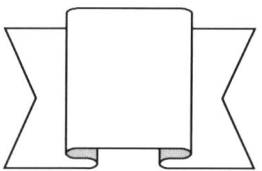

Tip 74

Practice good hygiene and be presentable.

Shampoo your hair and brush your teeth regularly. Wear clean clothes and deodorant.

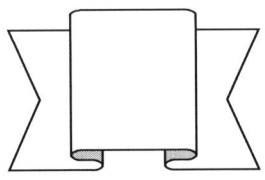

Tip 75

Don't text him too much.

If you text him, keep your texts interesting but not excessive. Too many texts can be annoying.

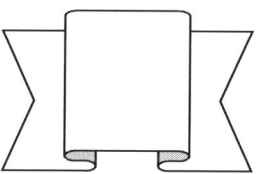

Tip 76

Try to make friends with a guy's ex-girlfriend.

This may help you avoid too much negative attention from a man's ex.

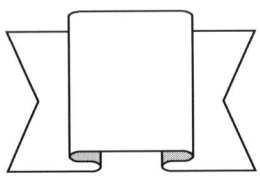

Tip 77

Have a genuine interest in a guy beyond his looks or his activities.

Get to know the real person.

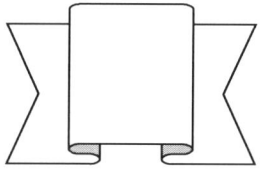

101 Flirting Tips for Women and Girls

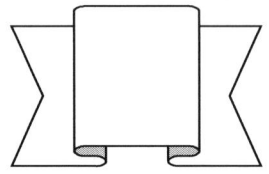

Chapter 10

How to Overcome Shyness Around a Guy You Like

101 Flirting Tips for Women and Girls

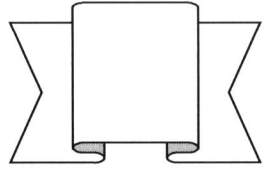

Tip 78

You can overcome your shyness.

You don't have to just sit there and watch other women attract a guy's attention.

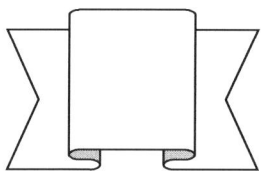

Tip 79

Just fake it.

Act like you are confident in yourself and you will look confident. You will need to psyche yourself up for this, but it becomes easier each time that you act cool and confident.

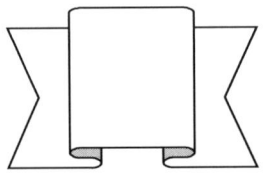

Tip 80

Practice smiling.

Smile at a guy and you will often reduce some of his nervousness as well as your own.

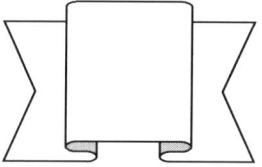

Tip 81

Walk over and say hello.

It's just a greeting and it lets a guy know that you have noticed him.

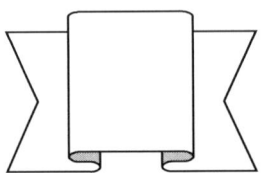

Tip 82

Think of things to say in advance.

After greeting him, see if he seems open to having a conversation and then just start talking.

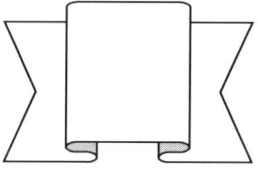

Tip 83

Complimenting him is a good way to get him interested in having a conversation.

You can say that you like his hair, cologne or clothes.

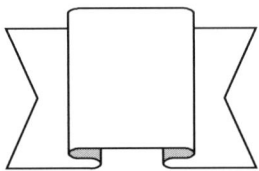

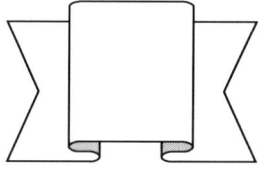

101 Flirting Tips for Women and Girls

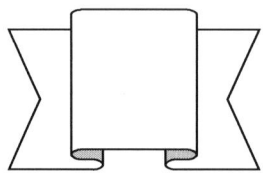

Chapter 11

How to Flirt and Drive a Guy Wild

101 Flirting Tips for Women and Girls

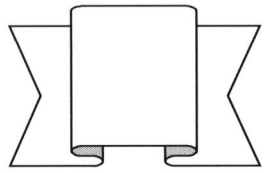

Tip 84

Use your eyelashes.

Batting your eyelashes as you glance at a guy can stop him in his tracks. Check out your eyelashes in the mirror and practice batting them. You may want to enhance your eyelashes to make them even more attractive.

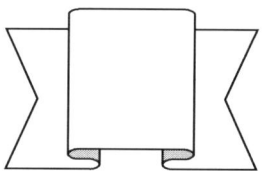

Tip 85

Practice different looks with your eyes.

Try to develop that dreamy look or a warm glowing glance combined with a smile. Position yourself to look straight at a guy or glance at him from the side.

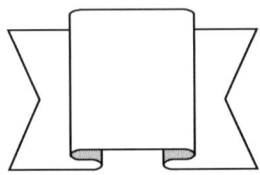

Tip 86

Use your lips.

Bite your lower lip as you look at a guy. Lick your lips with your tongue. Leave your lips parted just a little bit.

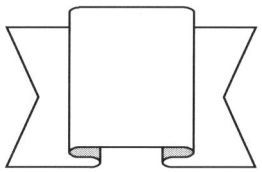

Tip 87

Touch a guy, but be subtle.

Briefly touch his arm, back or shoulder with your hand. Pretend he has a piece of lint on his clothes and remove it. Run your fingers through his hair if you are a little more daring.

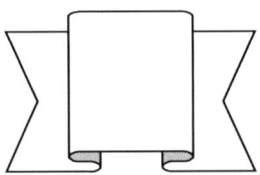

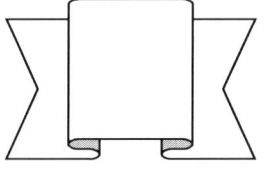

101 Flirting Tips for Women and Girls

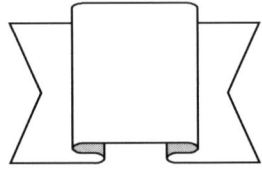

Chapter 12

Dress for Success When You Want to Flirt

101 Flirting Tips for Women and Girls

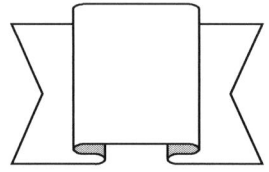

Tip 88

Wear skin tight clothes to show off your figure.

Wear a bikini if you are at the beach.

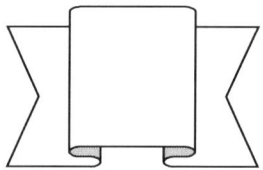

Tip 89

Put on your high heels to draw attention to your legs.

Your shoes can give your legs a more feminine appearance.

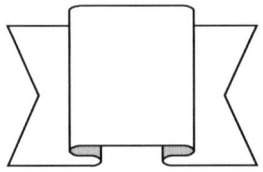

Tip 90

Use makeup for flirting.

Lip gloss, mascara and a light eye shadow can help enhance your look as you try to attract the attention of a man.

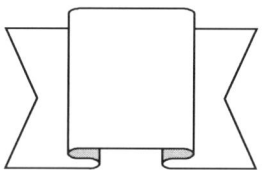

Tip 91

Choose a good perfume to lure a guy.

Spray some perfume on your wrists, neck and the insides of your elbows before you go out.

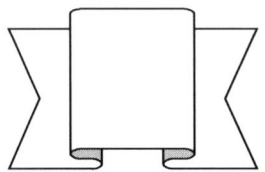

Tip 92

Choose your accessories.

Shiny and sparkly accessories are good flirting accessories. Necklaces, earrings and rings all help to attract guys, but don't overdo it. Bring a good looking purse or clutch.

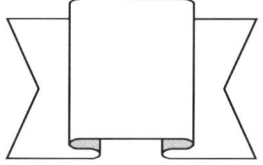

101 Flirting Tips for Women and Girls

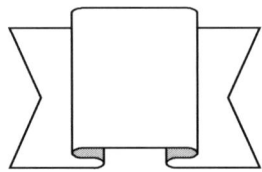

Chapter 13

Where to Flirt

There are many different places where you can find guys to flirt with.

101 Flirting Tips for Women and Girls

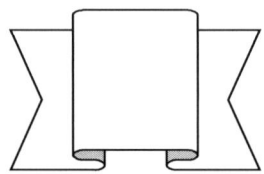

Tip 93

Flirt while commuting.

Strike up a conversation with a guy on the train or bus in the morning as you go to work or school. Flirt with a man on the commute home as well for a more relaxed environment.

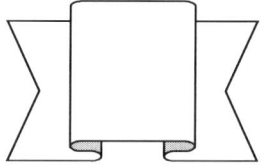

Tip 94

Check out guys at the bookstore.

You can find out about a man's interests by noticing the types of books he is interested in.

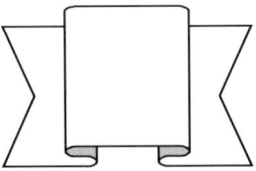

Tip 95

Coffee shops are great for meeting guys.

Lots of men like to sit in comfortable chairs in a coffee shop and read a newspaper, magazine or book.

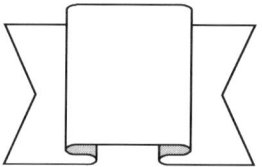

Tip 96

Sporting events are a fun place to meet guys.

Flirt with men who are on their way to the concession stands. Be discreet and be careful about distracting guys for too long during an important game.

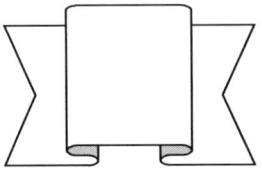

Tip 97

Meet guys at college or night school.

Strike up a conversation with a guy in your class about the subject matter of your course. Check out guys who are studying in the library or working in a computer lab.

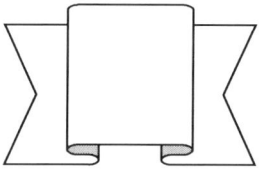

101 Flirting Tips for Women and Girls

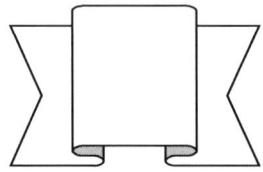

Chapter 14

Tips for Flirting Appropriately for Your Age

101 Flirting Tips for Women and Girls

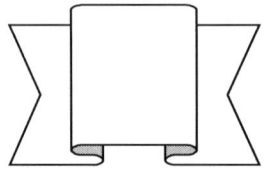

Tip 98

Twenties: Dress with the latest look. Talk about the latest hot topics for younger adults.

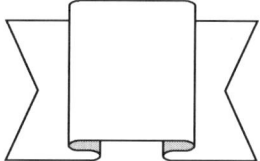

Tip 99

Thirties and Forties: Discuss your career and your latest job. Talk about your home or apartment. Discuss your new car if you bought one recently. Tell stories about your past love history but don't complain or be bitter.

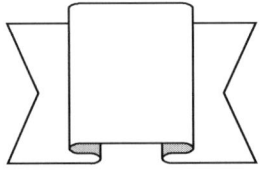

Tip 100

Fifties and Sixties: Discuss your grown children if you have any. Talk about their college lives or their careers. Talk about your grandchildren or other child relatives. Show off pictures of them and talk about how you spoil them.

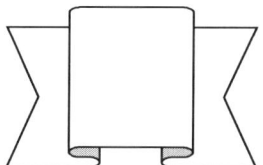

Tip 101

Seventies and Eighties: Discuss what you are doing to stay in good health. Talk about your traveling and the exercises you like to do. Look back on your life and talk about your accomplishments. Discuss the different places you have lived and what you liked about each place.

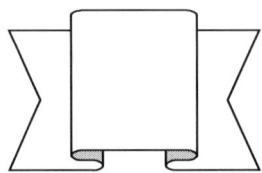

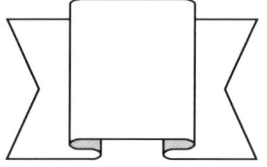

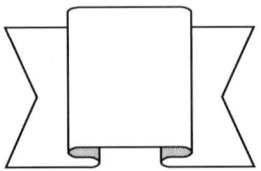

EXTRA HOT INFORMATION

Extra Tips on Flirting, Dating and Relationships

101 Flirting Tips for Women and Girls

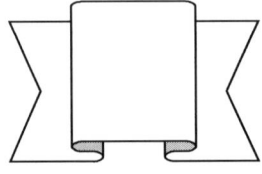

More Hot Tips

Get MORE HOT tips on flirting, dating and relationships. I have a special online resource section for you with updated information and the latest tips.

Visit www.ShawnBurnsBooks.com/tips-for-women

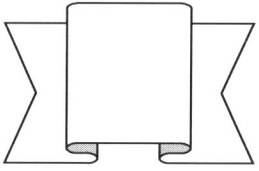

Printed in Great Britain
by Amazon